The Pitbull Dog Breed

A Comprehensive Pitbull Owner's Manual, Including Breed Specific Pitbull Training Techniques

by Edward Stenson

Table of Contents

Introduction 1

Chapter I: Your Dog Is Unique 7

Chapter II: Your Best Friend and Exercise 11

Chapter III: Your Pitbull and Its Social Behavior 15

Chapter IV: The Importance of Nutrition 19

Chapter V: Training Your Pitbull 23

Chapter VI: Commands and Tricks to Teach Your Dog 27

Conclusion..35

Introduction

The pitbull is probably the most misunderstood dog breed of all, but it is true that if not properly trained, it can be one of the most dangerous. Dogs have evolved alongside humans for thousands of years, having been essential to our survival.

Man has bred dogs for various jobs: for hunting small animals like rabbits, retrieving game that was killed over a long distance, herding livestock, and many others. Each dog breed has its own personality, and this is especially true when it comes to the pitbull. The pitbull is a descendant of mastiffs, bulldogs, and terriers and was specifically bred to be a big dog for hunting and fighting. Hunters would use them to hunt livestock and to catch semi-wild cattle and hogs. These dogs are so strong, they would take on bigger animals, like bulls and bears, by aiming for the prey's face and neck. This is why when you hear stories in the news about pitbull attacks, the report would usually say that they lunged for the victim's face and neck.

Pitbulls are misunderstood because the public generally believes that they're all dangerous. Although it is true that pitbulls can be dangerous if not trained properly, this is the case with all if not most dogs. Even though pitbulls are likely to be aggressive due to their genetic makeup, this doesn't mean that they *will* be. If trained properly, they can be among the sweetest dogs in the world. In this book, we will discuss this amazing breed and take a look at how we can train them into well-behaved companions for all.

Chapter I: Your Dog Is Unique

People often make the mistake of assuming that dogs of the same breed all act the same. Dog owners who pay attention to their pets realize that nothing could be further from the truth. Each dog has their own personality, just like humans. And just like humans, dogs have fears. Dogs know how to love as well, as studies show that dogs truly do love their masters. This is why dogs are able to emotionally bond with humans so well.

While humans are adept at hiding emotions, dogs can't help but show theirs. When happy, a dog will wag their tail, prick up their ears, jump around, and let loose a bark or two. If a dog is sad, they will tuck their tail between the legs, lower their back, and start to whine. When angry, a dog will bare their teeth and raise their back to signal that they are about to pounce. Dog emotions are currently being studied further, but just as dogs can understand many of our emotions, most pet owners also have a general understanding of a lot of the emotions their pets display.

Because all dogs are unique, you, as the dog owner, are in the best position to observe your dog and understand what their actions mean. It doesn't take long to figure out what makes them happy, what makes them sad, and what makes them angry. Pay close attention to what triggers anger early on, as knowing this could help prevent any future disasters. Look out for certain cues from your dog that could indicate that they are feeling threatened or caught in a bad situation. These cues include stiff posture, growling, or snapping. When you see these signs, make sure to calm down your dog before the situation escalates. Do this with soothing praise, by moving away from what might be causing the agitation, or taking your dog out for a walk.

Some dogs are highly intelligent and have high anxiety levels. This often results in a dominant personality. These dogs are often the pack leaders. Some people believe that dogs with this kind of personality will try to assert that dominance over their humans as well, since dogs tend to see us as their social peers. This is why you should always show dominance over your dog (which will be elaborated upon later in this book). If you have a pitbull with a dominant personality, you will need to show them who is boss without getting physical.

However, dominant dogs are a rarity, since you can only have one dominant dog per pack. Hence, when a pitbull is not cooperating with their owner, it is not usually because the dog is trying to assert dominance. It is more likely because the dog doesn't trust their master as they should. When a dog doesn't feel secure with their surroundings or the person they're with, they could either retreat fearfully or charge aggressively. In other breeds, this fear will be more obvious. Pitbulls, on the other hand, tend to channel their fear through aggression, as they are genetically predisposed to attack when under pressure.

Chapter II: Your Best Friend and Exercise

Like humans, dogs need lots and lots of exercise. However, unlike many of us, dogs are much more enthusiastic about it. We can liken dogs to a machine with energy levels that are continuously rising. You have to redirect all that pent-up energy that was bred into them for fighting and hunting into non-aggressive forms of activity. It's better for them to release this energy using their legs rather than with their teeth.

Pitbulls must be exercised every day. It is ideal to have a large lawn wherein the dog can play freely. It is a mistake, however, to think that you can just leave your dog in the yard to play on their own. The best way to exercise your dog is to exercise *with* them. They will be much more active when playing with their owner. Occasionally take your dog out to explore new environments too, as it will also exercise and sharpen their senses.

Throughout history, dogs hunted along humans, defended their humans, cared for their offspring, and played with each other. You can imagine that all those tasks require a lot of energy. The pitbull's genetic make-up, which is designed to do all that, has not changed—although we certainly don't send them out to hunt and defend much anymore. This should help us understand how they've come to have such a huge amount of pent-up energy. If a dog owner doesn't provide the right venue through which a pitbull can channel that energy, they will end up directing it toward the things you value, such as your furniture.

There are times when it will be hard to train and exercise your dog, like on days with bad weather. This will require a bit of creativity but it can be done. You can teach your dog to exercise using a treadmill, if you have one at home, for example. You can also let them go up and down the stairs a few times as exercise.

There are so many benefits to exercising your dog. Exercise reduces digestive problems, keeps your dog's weight under control, makes them go to sleep faster, and increases their overall longevity. Adult pitbulls are sometimes prone to developing bone diseases such as hip dysplasia and arthritis. Regular exercise starting at an early age can help prevent these awful health conditions when they are older.

Exercising your dog is not only healthy for them; it is also healthy for you. People who don't own dogs walk an average of 168 minutes per week, but people who own dogs walk about 130 minutes more per week. This shows dog owners are generally healthier. An added perk is the strengthening bond between you and your dog as you exercise together, which translates to increased loyalty and devotion.

When you are exercising with your dog, don't expect them to be able to do the same thing that you do. Dogs are short-distance runners, whereas humans can run for longer periods of time. If you decide to go jogging and take your dog out with you, don't expect your dog to last as long as you do, more so with pitbulls. Also, don't jog on hot days, as dogs can't release heat the same way people do by sweating so they get hot faster than humans. They also may have trouble breathing properly, especially if they happen to be breeds with flat faces or upturned snouts. Consider your dog's age when defining how much or how little exercise to give. Adult dogs may be able to make long runs, but not puppies. Puppies' bones are not fully developed, and too much running may cause their bones to grow in an unnatural way.

Lastly, consider swimming as another form of exercise for your pet. If you have a pool or live near a body of water, allow your dog to swim at least once a month. Dogs can instinctively swim, but you should still gradually introduce your pitbull pup to water. The best way to "break" your puppy into swimming is to accompany them in the water and have them first wade in the shallow parts. Don't force them into the deep end too soon, or you will risk drowning them. The same applies if you are swimming with your dog at a beach or in a lake.

Chapter III: Your Pitbull and Its Social Behavior

Pitbulls have the genetic make-up of fighters, with their bodies built to be aggressive. However, they don't necessarily have to be like that. Like any other breed, you can and must train your pitbull pups to be social. You may have to train them harder than other breeds, but it can be done.

You have to teach them to be social in their early years, because it gets harder as they get older. If you have a dog that wasn't socially trained early on, then you will probably need to keep it leashed in public at all times. Even if you think your adult pitbull is nice most of the time, pitbulls are built for aggression; therefore the possibility that it will act out is always present. Keeping your dog on a leash guarantees their own safety as well.

As a general rule, pitbulls that have not been socially trained when they were young should not be brought to dog parks. Going to dog parks with adult pitbulls, even if they were socially trained from the start, can be challenging. However, that does not mean that older dogs *can't* be taught. If you have an adult pitbull that wasn't socialized, it isn't too late to help them become social. It will certainly be harder to train them, but it's possible and necessary nonetheless.

When you are socializing your pitbull pup, make sure that they spend time around other dogs as much as possible. The best way to do this is to have more than one dog around your pitbull pup at all times. 'Play dates' with other dogs of different breeds will allow your pet to feel like it is part of a pack. In social settings, let your pup sniff other dogs' behinds, as this is a way of social introduction among canines. A good sign that the dogs are socializing is if they're relaxed and are not making eye contact with each other. If you find that one of the dogs is stiffening up around your pitbull, or vice versa, then remove your pitbull from the pack. You can re-introduce your pitbull at a later time.

If you can't or don't want to own more than one dog, use daily walks to get your pitbull acquainted with other dogs. Put your dog on a leash and walk in neutral territory with another dog owner. Make sure that your dogs are a good distance away from each other. This will ensure that there is no fighting between the two dogs. Don't be fooled by how friendly they look walking side by side, as it only takes a second for a vicious fight to start between a pitbull and another dog. There will also be times when your dog will want to venture off and do their own thing. You will have to show dominance in these situations and tug the leash every time your dog attempts to stray away from you.

Your pitbulls need to be trained to be social not just with other dogs but with other people as well. Your dog is more likely to be around another human being than with another dog, so you have to make sure that your dogs are well-behaved with both. If you have children, you should wait until a pitbull is properly trained before introducing them to each other. If you are raising a pitbull pup from infancy, then the pup can safely be around your children all the time with adult supervision. However, you must make sure that your pitbull treats your kids just as they treat you.

After this, your dogs will have to learn how to behave among other people that they do not see every day. In these cases, you should make sure that your dog is leashed and under control. Don't allow just anyone to walk up to your dog and pet them: That's a recipe for disaster.

If a stranger wants to pet your dog, tell them that they will have to avoid eye contact with your dog, and you'll have to let the dog sniff their legs. Only when your pitbull is accustomed to the new person can the person move in slowly and pet them gently. It's good to remember to take things slowly with all dogs, especially with an aggressive breed such as this.

As a final note on pitbull socialization, know that there are some dogs that are born aloof and thus, will not thrive as well in social situations. Like humans, all dogs have their own personalities. Conversely, some pitbulls will always get too excited around other dogs, so you will have to monitor them constantly. You will just have to know your dog well enough to know what to do in certain situations.

Chapter IV: The Importance of Nutrition

Because of the level of energy pitbulls have, they will need high-calorie meals to carry them through the day. Don't think you need to break the bank to feed your dogs, however.

In the puppy stages, pets need to be fed the best food for good growth. Avoid giving your puppies human food or leftovers; give it dry and wet dog food instead. Pitbull puppies will need 5 ½ cups of dry food or 1 ½ cans of wet food combined with 3 cups of dry food per day. According to the Dog Breed Information Center, this food should be divided over two meals each day. Ensure that your puppies are eating at regular intervals. Have a set time for breakfast and dinner each day, as this will prevent digestive problems like constipation and diarrhea. Your dog should be drinking as much as they eat. Water is actually more essential than food, as dehydration will kill quicker than hunger. Keep food and drink bowls clean and fresh throughout the day, and use filtered water instead of tap water when you can.

Treats are a nice thing to give your dog, but they can interrupt with your dog's digestion. Give treats only when needed, like during training. In order for treats to be effective, you can't be free-feeding them to your dog throughout the day. Ensure that the meal times are set, and that when you present a treat, they are hungry enough to eat it. Do not overfeed with treats and snacks, since overfeeding will spoil their meals. Your dogs should have the same feeding schedule in adulthood as when they were puppies. If you don't stick to a regular eating time, dogs stand to risk obesity and other health complications.

Another food option to consider for your dog is raw food. A lot of chemicals and preservatives are packed in the dry and wet dog food that is sold in your average supermarket or pet store. With fresh raw food, your pets are more likely to get the nutrients that they need, like protein, roughage, and vitamins. A raw food dish would usually have chicken, beef, steak, pork, and fish. While raw foods are generally more nutritious, it is only recommended for older dogs, so do not even think about feeding raw food to your puppies. Keep in mind that feeding natural raw food increases the chance that your dog will grow more aggressive. If you don't want overly aggressive pitbulls, stick to the food that is sold in paper bags and cans.

Lastly, you can always choose to go the homemade route. When you cook for your dog, the dog will more likely get more of the nutrients they need, since the meal is more properly planned. It is also more economical than buying dog food from a store. This method is *not* the same as feeding your dog with human food scraps. Your dog needs a well-balanced meal, and table scraps are rarely well-balanced. If you decide to cook for your dog, make sure that there is adequate protein and vegetables. Starches such as rice, corn, and wheat are filling for humans but are not really important for dogs.

Chapter V: Training Your Pitbull

The first step in training any animal is teaching discipline. Discipline is the ability to put aside one's own desires and natural behaviors in order to complete a task. If an animal is not disciplined, they will not follow your orders. Take yourself for example: When you need to complete a task, whether it is at work or at home, you need a disciplined mind to complete it. Someone without discipline would probably slack off. Sometimes we reward ourselves when a task is completed, which is referred to as the positive reinforcement technique. You will have to take the same approach in training your pitbulls. Sometimes negative reinforcement is also called for, but it is best to use positive reinforcement techniques when training your pitbull pups.

So, how does one use positive reinforcement to train their dog? Consider yourself and the way you get things done using positive reinforcement. What treats or rewards do you give yourself? Chocolate? Ice cream? Netflix? The same mentality applies when training your puppy. Of course, dogs are intolerant of chocolate, and they are not all that likely to enjoy *House of Cards* either, so think about the things your dog likes. Belly rubs? Runs in the park? A ride in the car? Doggy treats? When you have identified your dog's likes, use them to your advantage during training.

However you decide to train your dog, you must always make sure that it knows that you are their master and assert your dominance. Be firm and don't fall for the puppy-eye look. Let your pup know that they must obey you at all times. Dogs, like wolves, are social creatures, and wolf packs will always have a leader. You must establish that you are the leader of the pack. The first step in establishing your dominance is to praise it when it does something right, but take care not to give it too much praise. Praise lasting 5 to 10 seconds is ideal for a good deed. Drag it out any longer and you have a spoiled pup. On the opposite end, you should also dish out quick punishment when your pitbull does something wrong. Like your praise, do not punish your dog for more than 10 seconds; around 5 seconds is more ideal. Don't resort to striking your dogs, as this can provoke an act of aggression. You can assert your dominance by locking them away in a kennel, or leashing them into one position. Dogs like to be free, so you will get the idea through to them quickly if you restrict their freedom.

Nothing is worse than having a dog urinate and defecate wherever they want, especially when that dog is more often inside the house than outside. You have to house-train your pups from the start to ensure that they relieve themselves in a designated area. Dogs don't defecate just anywhere; they often go back to the place where they relieved themselves before. You can use this same instinctive behavior to your advantage. To do this, pick a spot where they can relieve themselves. Line it with eye-catching material, like colored rocks, that the dog will notice every time. Then, work out a schedule when to bring the dog out to relieve themselves. A pitbull puppy will need to go once every 2-4 hours a day. Bring them to the designated spot and make sure that they relieve themselves there before bringing them back. Eventually, the dog will learn to go to the same spot on their own to pee or to poop.

Do not let your pitbull pups bite you. It may be cute, but puppies grow up. And when they are grown, it won't be so cute anymore. When a pup bites you, react negatively by saying no without striking them. This will make the dog realize that they shouldn't bite you or any other human. You can provide your pet chew toys, since dogs, especially pitbulls, love to chew things. Chew toys will prevent them from ruining your furniture, shoes, and other valued items around your house as well.

Finally, do not allow your pitbulls to walk around the neighborhood freely, even when they are harmless pups. Train your dog to get used to the leash, as it is never too early to teach self-control. Your dog is also within your reach when leashed, so it also allows you to monitor them more effectively. When using a leash, check that you don't buckle it too tight, or else you will hurt the dog. Because your dog will often try to go their own way, you should learn how to direct them by tugging on the leash without choking them. Also remember to validate your pet with praise whenever they do the right thing when you go on your walking sessions.

Chapter VI: Commands and Tricks to Teach Your Dog

You will need to get those previously mentioned treats ready to train and teach your dogs new tricks. Don't think you can depend on treats alone, however. Treats should only be used in the first few repetitions of teaching your dog a new trick. After that, you should make sure that your dog obeys your vocal and gestural commands even without treats. It's best to have your pup on a leash and make it face you the whole time. Your dog may act up at times, so you have to be able to control situations caused by this often erratic and aggressive breed. Here are some basic tricks that teach discipline:

Sit

This is the first trick you will teach your dog before progressing to other tricks. The 'sit' trick will also give you some control when your pitbull decides to act up. To train your dog to sit, make them stand in attention facing you. Put a treat in front of their nose, about a few inches away, and then slowly move the treat up above their head. The pup will move their head up to track the treat, and when their head cannot go up any further while standing, they will sit. Once it does that, reward the dog with praise and the treat. After this, make your dog stand up again and repeat the whole process, but this time, repeat the word "sit" while moving the treat above their head. Do this several times. Afterwards, use the same hand motions but without the treat in your hand. Reward your dog with a treat only when they follow your command. Eventually, replace your treats with just simple praise. It is more effective when you don't touch or push your dog's back to teach them how to sit.

Down

If you want your dog to stop jumping up on your house guests, then you should teach them how to follow the "down" command. In this second trick, you will be able to make them lie down on your command. First, command your dog to sit. When it does, praise them but don't give them any treats. From that sitting position, hold a treat in front of them, and repeat the word "down." While doing so, move the treat down and make sure the dog is following it with their nose. Bring it close to the ground, and start moving it away from the dog at that low level. The dog will tend to ease itself into a lying down position with their elbows on the floor. When this happens, reward your dog with a treat and praise. Motion to your dog to sit, and repeat several more times. After this, without the treat in your hand, repeat the verbal command "down" while using the same hand motions you did previously, and as soon as your dog gets into the down position, reward with a treat and praise. Remember once a dog learns a trick, you should reduce the number of treats you give until you can stop rewarding them with treats altogether.

Stand

Suppose you don't want to have to stoop down to give your dog a high five? Well, you can teach it to stand! This may be the easiest of all the tricks, since dogs can stand without you having to teach them how. However, tricks are more about the dog appropriately responding to your command than simply executing certain actions by themselves. To start, have a treat in one hand and let your dog lie down in front of you. Remember to keep the treat out of sight. Using hand gestures and a voice command, order your dog to stand. It may take a while and you may have to get your body into it a little, but your dog will eventually get the idea. Once they do, let your dog rest their paws on your abdomen and praise them while rewarding them with the hidden treat. Repeat the previous steps about five more times for your dog to know that in order for it to receive a treat, they will have to stand when the "stand" gestures and commands are given.

There may be times when your dog will stand up without your signal, so make it clear that the dog will get a treat only when they stand on command. After five repetitions, move away from the dog when they stand so they don't lean on your abdomen. Keep signaling for them to stand if they get back on all fours. If your dog manages to stand up on their own for more than a second, then give them a treat and praise. Repeat this 3-5 times.

Come

This is a trick that your dog will learn very quickly. Have your dog sit down, and praise them when they do so. Move about 10 feet away and hold a treat out while using your other hand to beckon to them. Reward them with a treat and praise if they get up to move to you. Repeat the previous steps, making them sit while you walk away, but this time, call your dog by name and give the vocal command to "come". If your dog's name is Rufus, say "Rufus, come." Make sure you're gesturing with your hand to beckon as well. If your dog obeys, reward them with a treat again. Repeat for about 5 times. After that, beckon them to come but without the hand signals for another 5 repetitions. Finally, make them come with voice commands without the aid of any treats.

Stay

This is a simple trick that doesn't rely too much on treats. It's best to teach the "stay" trick outdoors while your dog is leashed. Start by commanding your dog to sit. As usual, give praise if they obey. Next, while walking backwards, hold out your hand and say "stay." Keep repeating the command as you walk farther and farther away from them. Once you're at a good distance, stop and beckon your dog to come to you. Give your dog a treat when they come. Walk your dog back to the original position and repeat the steps above. If your dog doesn't come the first time, shorten the distance between you.

Your relationship with your dog grows deeper as you master these basic tricks. Having mastered these will give you the confidence to try your hand at the "party" tricks below:

High Five

One of the easiest tricks to teach a dog is the "high five." Start with the dog in "sit" position. Stoop down to their eye-level or sit on the floor, and place a treat in front of them just out of their reach. Slightly elevate one of your dog's feet with one of your hands while saying "high five." Do this repeatedly until they completely raise their foot by themselves. Once they do this, grab the foot with your other hand and reward them with the treat. Do this as often as you need to, and if done right, the dog will learn to raise their paw just by seeing you raise your hand in front of them.

Roll Over

This is another trick that is a must-learn for dogs everywhere. This one is a bit more difficult than sit and stand, but the result is very rewarding. First, make sure that your dog is lying down. Then, hold out a treat in front of them and move the treat to the side and a little above their head to signal that the dog should roll on their side. You may have to gently prod and guide your pet while doing this. Don't stop until you successfully get them on their side. Proceed to use the treat to make them roll their back, then to their other side, and then back to their belly. Reward them with a treat, but know that the process is only just beginning. This trick will normally require many repetitions and you may have to guide your pup again. Keep on repeating the gestures until they roll over by themselves without you having to use a treat. Once your dog starts rolling over, start using the voice command along with the treat. You must also signal with your hand using a circular motion. Remember to reward them with praise and a treat when your dog does the trick without prodding.

Play Dead

This trick may seem hard, and it is, but if your dog has already learned to roll over, then "play dead" will be a breeze. First, get them to lie down just like you did with the "roll over" trick. To make sure your dog remembers, do the roll over trick about 3-5 times. When your dog is all warmed up, say "play dead" while using your fingers to form the shape of a gun. Your dog won't know what to do here, so immediately signal for them to roll over. If they do, stop them when their legs are in the air by rubbing their belly. Let them return to the first position again, and give the "play dead" voice command with the gun fingers. Immediately give the signal to roll over again, and ensure that they stop on their back. When you are signaling them to roll over while teaching them to play dead, it is best to use the "roll over" hand gestures only without the "roll over" voice command. Keep repeating these steps. After about 5 times, stop doing the "roll over" command. They will know by this time to roll on their back every time you say "play dead" and make gun fingers. When they successfully play dead, reward them with a treat.

Conclusion

The public needn't be more afraid of pitbulls than any other breed. The truth is that any breed of dog can be bred to develop dangerous characteristics, just as they can be trained to be sociable. It should also be noted that the news about pitbulls mauling their owners or other people is usually due to some neglect on the part of the owners themselves. If pitbulls are trained in the manner we discussed in this guide, they can be controlled and thus, there should be no need to fear them.

Remember too that pitbulls that are chained outdoors and separated from their owners will always display higher acts of aggression. This is because that is how pitbulls were treated back when they were hunting dogs used to take down bulls and bears. When more dog owners take responsibility in training their pitbulls well, the public will also change its perception of this beautiful breed. Maybe then, the law will also start to focus less on the ownership of these dogs and more on people's actions when owning them.

Just like people, all dogs are individuals and have their own distinctive personalities. We don't treat every person the same based on their race or characteristics they were born with, so we should not treat all dogs the same, especially infamous breeds like pitbulls. Take the time to know and understand your own dog's likes and habits. It takes a master's love to see which of the different training approaches they will respond best to. When you invest the time and love required, you will be rewarded with the most loyal and loving companion you've ever had!

Finally, I'd like to thank you for purchasing this book! If you enjoyed it or found it helpful, I'd greatly appreciate it if you'd take a moment to leave a review on Amazon. Thank you!

51865794R00024

Made in the USA
San Bernardino, CA
03 August 2017